PART ONE
THE RISE OF THE FASCISTS

Rome 1935: Fascist soldiers march past the statue
of Augustus Casear, one of the greatest of the ancient Roman emperors

On 17 March 1861 a new country was born after years of struggle and fighting – the Kingdom of Italy. Italians throughout the country were very excited. For over a thousand years, ever since the fall of the Roman Empire, they had been a divided people living in separate small states. Now that they were united once more, many Italians began to think they would become powerful again, as they had been in the time of the Romans. The Pope summed up their feelings when he said this to an English visitor in 1861:

> 'Do you know what Italian unity means? It means a nation of five and twenty millions harbouring more talent, more mind and more energy than any nation in the world. Italy left to herself would soon be the first of the great powers of the world.'

You might not agree with what the Pope said about the Italian people. You may think that your own nation has more talent, more mind and more energy than any other country. But whatever your own opinion, it is important to understand the Italian opinion as well. To help you see their point of view, try doing the quiz opposite.

After doing the quiz you will probably agree that many famous names of the past are Italian names. This is partly what the Pope was getting at. Perhaps also he was thinking about how the Italian people have affected the way other nations have developed. Many of the languages spoken in the world today come from the language of the ancient Italians, Latin. And much of our law is also based on that of the ancient Italians.

It was for reasons like these that the Pope and millions of other Italians had high hopes for their future when the country was united in 1861. They had been great in the past; why should they not become even greater in the future?

This book tells the story of how Italy did become a 'great power' under the rule of Benito Mussolini and his Fascist Party. But it did not happen as quickly as the Pope predicted in 1861, and it was only achieved at the cost of great bloodshed and suffering.

THE PROBLEMS OF ITALY

At the start of the twentieth century the Kingdom of Italy was far from being 'the first of the great powers of the world'. During the forty years after unification, all sorts of major problems had developed.

The problem of the South

The southern half of Italy was very poor in comparison with the North. Four out of five people in the South could not read or write. Disease and early death were common and unemployment was high. There were areas in Sicily and Sardinia where the people lived for months on end on nothing but wild plants. Because they were so poor the people of the South often rebelled. In 1893 groups of workers calling themselves *Fasci* rioted so violently that the government had to put the whole island of Sicily under siege.

The entrance to a sulphur mine in Sicily at the end of the nineteenth century. Nearly 100 per cent of sulphur miners had tuberculosis

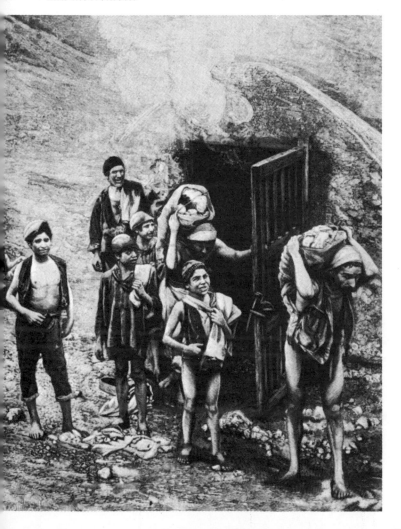

Italy in 1900: this map shows places mentioned in this book. Note that Sardinia and Sicily are part of Italy

Political problems

In theory the Kingdom of Italy was a democracy, with regular elections and a parliament. In practice the political system was corrupt and inefficient. Very few people had the right to vote and anyway elections were usually rigged by the government. One Italian politician described elections like this:

> 'The police enrolled the scum of the underworld. . . . In the last weeks before the polls the opponents were threatened, clubbed, besieged in their homes. Their leaders were prevented from attending meetings, or even thrown into prison until election day was over. Voters favouring government candidates were given not only their own voting cards, but also those of opponents, emigrants and deceased voters, and were allowed to vote three, ten, twenty times.'

In parliament itself the members often fought with one another and the Chairman was sometimes showered with paper darts. To get support for their policies, government ministers usually had to bribe members of parliament with money, jobs or business contracts.

For all these reasons, few Italians had much confidence in their system of government, and many were prepared to use violence against it.

The problem of the Pope

Before Italy was united the Pope ruled large areas of land in central Italy called the Papal States. When Italy was united the new government took the Pope's land away from him and left him with only a small area of Rome to rule, the Vatican. The Pope therefore disliked the government and did not want it to win the support of the people. He banned all Italian Catholics from voting in elections and from being members of parliament.

Since most Italians were Catholics, millions obeyed the Pope's ban. This meant that they never got to understand or like the system of democracy under which they lived. The Pope ended his ban in 1905 but by that time the damage had been done. Nearly a whole generation of Italians had grown up ignorant of politics and suspicious of politicians.

Economic problems

On the surface, many parts of Italy looked prosperous. In 1900 the Fiat car company was set up and by 1913 was exporting 4000 cars a year. Great dams were being built on rivers in the Alps to provide hydro-electric power. Every year tourists flocked to Italy bringing valuable foreign currency with them.

But beneath the surface much of Italy was very poor. Half the population made its living by farming, but there was not enough land for everyone. Seventeen million farm workers worked for five million landowners and there was frequent fighting between them over wages, rents and working conditions. In some years, whole provinces of Italy were in a state of near-warfare when fights broke out between the landowners and their farm workers.

In the towns as well as the countryside there was discontent and violence. As industry grew, so did the

An Italian family with all their belongings arrives on Ellis Island in New York harbour, 1905

slums. Workers readily joined political parties like the Socialists or Anarchists who promised to help them get better working conditions and wages. Hardly a year went by without riots and rebellions in the cities: in 1898 over a hundred people were killed when hunger riots broke out in Milan, and in 1904 there was a general strike in Italy.

Not surprisingly, many Italians tried to escape from their poverty by emigrating, mostly to America. About half a million left Italy on steamships every year, forming what some people called 'The Third Italy' abroad.

Work section

A. Study the drawing of sulphur miners in Sicily on the opposite page. Write down three things you notice about the people in the picture which tell you that they led hard lives.

B. Read the description on the opposite page of how Italian elections were rigged by the government.
1. Why would you call this sort of behaviour undemocratic?
2. Which of the government's attempts to rig elections seems to you the most unfair? Explain your answers.

C. 1. From which part of Italy do you think the family in the photograph above has come?
2. For what reasons might they have emigrated?
3. How might they have expected life in America to be better than life in Italy?

NEW IDEAS FOR ITALY'S FUTURE

As you have seen, Italy was suffering from major problems when the twentieth century began. This did not stop Italians from believing that one day their country would be great again. But it did make them realise that it would not happen by itself. All sorts of new ideas and plans for the future began to spread.

The Futurists

One group calling itself the **Futurists** thought that Italy would never become great while it had so much history behind it. They said that the Italians were so

'Terminal for aeroplanes and trains with funicular.' A futurist design of 1914

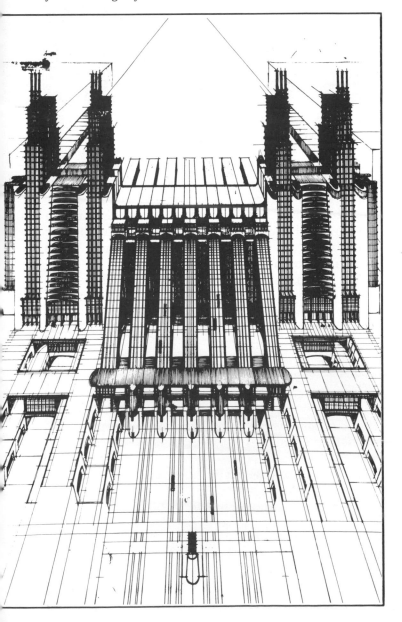

proud of their past that they had no desire to create a new future. Their plan was therefore to destroy the past. Filippo Marinetti, the leader of the group, wrote in *The Futurist Manifesto*: 'Set fire to the libraries! Divert canals to flood museums! Let the glorious paintings swim ashore! Undermine the foundations of ancient towns!' He warned the people of Venice that: 'Your Grand Canal, widened and dredged, will be turned into a bustling port.'

In place of ancient monuments and museums, the Futurists wanted to put up huge new buildings like the railway station in the drawing below left. Marinetti wanted the work of destruction to be done by young men of action, trained in special schools of physical courage. Above all, the Futurists believed that war and violence were good things. As Marinetti said on one occasion: 'Long live war, the world's best hygiene!'

The Nationalists

Another group also believed that war and violence would be needed to make Italy great. They were the **Nationalist Party**, set up in 1910. One of its leaders, Enrico Corradini, said: 'We shall never be a nation without a war!'

The Nationalists' strongest belief was that Italy was not a 'whole' country because parts of it were ruled by

Land that the Nationalists wanted

neighbouring countries. Look at the map on the previous page to see which areas they had in mind. Their aim was to get back these areas, by war if necessary, in order to make Italy complete. They also believed that Italy's poverty could be cured by conquering land in North Africa. Corradini said: 'Over there in Tripoli, millions of men could live happily.'

The Nationalists quickly became very popular. Millions supported them and, in 1912, the government did invade Tripoli and made it into an Italian colony, Libya.

The Socialists

A third group with new and violent ideas about how to change Italy was the **Socialist Party**. In 1914 they tried to overthrow the government in a revolution during what they called 'Red Week'. They seized control of the town of Ancona and made it into a socialist republic. In other parts of the country they overthrew local governments and organised a general strike.

The Socialists were defeated after only one week because the army was called in to deal with them. But although 'Red Week' was a failure, it did show how close Italy was to a violent revolution.

A chance for action

Not all Italians agreed with the new ideas that were spreading. Most thought the Futurists were simply mad. The Nationalists were considered by some to be too extreme. Many feared the Socialists because they were terrified of what might happen in a revolution.

Then, in August 1914, the chance came for some of the new ideas to be put to the test. War broke out in Europe and quickly spread to become the first world war – the Great War of 1914 – 18. This was the moment for which both the Futurists and the Nationalists had been waiting.

A postcard advertising a Socialist meeting in the city of Bologna in 1904. Karl Marx, the founder of socialism, is holding the red flag of socialism and trampling on the Pope. In the distance the sun of socialism is rising over Italy

Work section

A. Test your understanding of this chapter by answering these questions.
1. Why did Marinetti and the Futurists want to destroy Italy's ancient monuments and works of art?
2. Name the areas of land that the Nationalists wanted to get in order to make Italy 'whole'.
3. What kind of society do you think the Revolutionary Socialists hoped to create in Italy?
4. Why do you think the Futurists and the Nationalists believed that war and violence were needed to make Italy great?

B. Study the Socialist postcard above. Explain in your own words what you think the picture means. Then suggest some reasons why it may have made Italians suspicious of the Socialists.

C. Find a picture of a famous building or scene that you know well. It might be a beautiful area of countryside, an old building in the town where you live, or a national monument like Nelson's Column or the Houses of Parliament in London. Now do a drawing or write a description of this place as a Futurist would like it to be. Look at the picture on the opposite page to give yourself ideas about this.

D. Make notes to help you remember what you have read so far. Use points A and B of the revision guide on page 18 as a framework for your notes.

ITALY AT WAR

Italy did not join the Great War as soon as it started. For nine months the Italians argued furiously about whether they should or should not fight.

Attitudes to war

You have probably already guessed that the Nationalists and the Futurists wanted to go to war straight away. In fact some of them didn't wait for the government to declare war. Four thousand of them marched off to help the French by joining the French Foreign Legion.

But not everyone wanted war. More than anybody else the Socialists were against it. They thought that war could do nothing but harm to the working class as it was the workers who would have to do all the fighting. The cartoon opposite, which appeared in the Socialist newspaper *Avanti!* (meaning *Forward!*) in 1914 summed up their feelings on the matter.

The argument about joining the war split the Socialist Party in two, however. **Benito Mussolini**, one of the Party's leaders and editor of *Avanti!* was at first against Italy joining the war. Then his opinions began to change. These extracts from his newspaper articles show how he changed his mind:

> 'Down with the War! Down with arms and up with humanity!'   (26 July 1914)

> 'To offer the same kind of opposition to all wars . . . is stupidity bordering on the imbecile. Do you want to be spectators of this great drama? Or do you want to be its fighters?'   (10 October 1914)

Because he changed his mind Mussolini was thrown out of the Socialist Party. He set up his own newspaper, *Il Popolo d'Italia (The People of Italy)*, and began to write outspoken articles in favour of the war. In the first issue he wrote this:

> 'I address my first word to you, the young men of Italy, the young men of the factories and universities, the young men . . . to whom fate has given the task of making history. It is a word which in normal times I would never have used but which today I utter loudly and clearly, the fearful and fascinating word – War.'

Thousands of Socialists agreed with Mussolini's point of view and left the party to join him. Together, they joined the Nationalists in riots and demonstrations, trying to force the government to declare war. Eventually, on 26 April 1915, the Italian government made up its mind and declared war on Germany and Austria-Hungary.

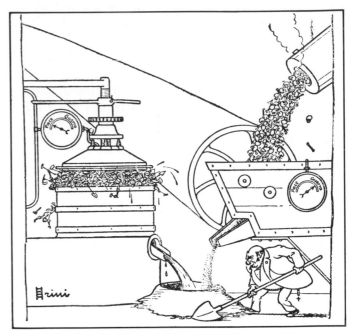

'From the blood of the workers and the bones of the soldiers, the capitalist prepares the cement to build his markets with'

The government did not decide to go to war because of Mussolini's riots and demonstrations. It did so because Britain and France made Italy an offer it could not refuse. At a secret meeting in London they signed a treaty, the secret **Treaty of London**, offering Italy large areas of land if she would fight on the side of Britain and France. The areas being offered were the Tyrol, Istria, Dalmatia and a number of islands in the

Italian soldiers fighting in the Alps

Italian soldiers retreating from the town of Caporetto in 1917

Mediterranean Sea. Look back to the map on page 4 and you should be able to work out why the Italian government was unable to resist their offer.

Within a month, workers and peasants were made to join the army and marched off to fight the Austrians.

Casualties

The secret Treaty of London did not seem such a good bargain once the fighting had started. To attack the Austrians, the Italians had to cross high mountain ranges and sometimes climb sheer cliffs while hidden Austrian soldiers fired down on them. They fought bravely, moving slowly forward on skis, roped together for safety. But every time they advanced they were beaten back. During two years of fighting they managed to get only 15 kilometres inside Austria. Then disaster struck. In October 1917 the Austrians sent their entire army to the Italian front. With the help of seven hand-picked German divisions, they forced the Italians to make a sudden retreat from the town of **Caporetto** (see map on page 2).

Although the Italians gained revenge a year later by beating the Austrians in the battle of **Vittorio Veneto**, they never forgot the retreat from Caporetto. The men who had thought that war would make their country great now felt only shame and humiliation.

Work section

A. Test your understanding of this chapter by answering these questions.
   1. When and why did the Italian government declare war on Germany and Austria?
   2. Which areas of land was Italy promised in the secret Treaty of London? Why do you think the Italian Nationalists were particularly pleased by this?
   3. When and why were the Italians defeated at the Battle of Caporetto?

B. Study the Socialist cartoon on the opposite page. Explain in your own words the message you think it is trying to put across.

C. Read the extracts from Mussolini's newspaper articles on the opposite page. Suggest reasons why he was in favour of joining the war even though he was a Socialist.

D. Look at the photograph of soldiers fighting in the Alps. Make a list of the difficulties they must have faced in fighting in these conditions.

E. Study the photograph of Italian soldiers retreating from Caporetto. How can you tell from the photograph that they have been defeated in battle and forced to retreat?

THE 'MUTILATED VICTORY'

In November 1918 the Germans and the Austrians surrendered and the Great War was over. Although Italy had been beaten at Caporetto she was on the winning side of the war, and now looked forward to the fruits of victory.

The cost of the war

The price that Italy had paid for victory was very high. Over 600,000 Italians were dead, 950,000 were wounded, and 250,000 were crippled for life.

The government had spent 148,000 million lire during the three years of fighting. This was double the amount it had spent in the 53 years since Italy was united.

The war also had serious effects on the country's economy. There was inflation, which meant that people's wages were losing their value. The war ruined trade, so Italy found it hard to sell her exports. This, in turn, led to unemployment.

Hopes for the peace

Despite the high cost of the war, many Italians believed that their suffering would be rewarded. In the last year of the war the government had made promises to the soldiers to keep up their fighting spirit. They had promised to give land to the peasants, to provide jobs for people in the cities, pensions for the families of the dead, and medical treatment for the wounded.

Many of the soldiers also felt that the fighting had been worthwhile because Italy would now get back the lands which belonged to her.

Dashed hopes

In 1919 160,000 soldiers returned from the war, filled with hope for the future. Their hopes were quickly dashed. Young soldiers could not get jobs because they had been called up to fight before they could learn a trade, so now they had no skills to offer employers. Wounded men found that there were long delays in getting pensions and medical treatment.

To make matters worse, Italy was not given all the land she had been promised by the secret Treaty of London. At the Peace Conference in Paris in 1919, the politicians did not seem to be very interested in Italy. Although they gave Tyrol and Istria to Italy, they gave Dalmatia to the new country of Yugoslavia. The Nationalists were furious. They felt they had been betrayed.

The soldiers who were most angry when they returned home were the *Arditi*. They were the

Wounded ex-soldiers of the Italian army demonstrate against the government in 1919

specially trained commando fighters of the army, famous for their daring and their ruthlessness. Dressed in black uniforms, they had taken the biggest risks and had faced death every day. Now, even Italy's heroes found themselves without jobs or rewards.

For all these reasons, people began to complain that although Italy was on the winning side of the war, she had won 'a mutilated victory'.

Fascism is born

During the cold winter months of early 1919 the *Arditi* formed themselves into organised groups. The first *Arditi* Association was set up in Rome by a Futurist. Marinetti, the leader of the Futurists, set up a National Association of the *Arditi* in Milan. The walls of its headquarters were draped with black flags painted with the skull and crossbones. Everywhere in the building were helmets, bayonets, rifles and especially daggers, their favourite weapon.

Arditi groups were set up throughout Italy in February 1919. They started a newspaper and began to grow strong.

Not all members of the *Arditi* Associations had been commandos in the war. One of them was Benito Mussolini, who, as you know, was thrown out of the Socialist Party in 1914 because he wanted Italy to join the war. Although he had joined the army and fought bravely, his army career was cut short in an accident when a cannon he was loading blew up, leaving forty pieces of metal embedded in his body.

At the end of the war, after his wounds had healed, Mussolini joined one of the *Arditi* Associations and became its leading member. But Mussolini wanted to go further and make the *Arditi* into armed fighting groups with himself as their leader. On 23 March 1919 he set up a **Fascio di Combattimento** (*Battle Group*) consisting of 119 men. Standing round a black flag they drew daggers from their belts, stretched out their arms in salute and swore this oath: 'We swear to defend Italy. For her we are prepared to kill and to die.'

The enemies of the Fascists

Why did Mussolini and his *Fasci* think it would be necessary to 'kill and die' for Italy?

Their main reason was fear of a communist revolution in Italy. Two years earlier, in 1917,

Mussolini in the army in 1916

Communists had overthrown the Russian government. In 1918 there had been an attempt at revolution in Germany. Now, in 1919, it seemed that communism was sweeping through all of Europe. Mussolini explained his fears in a speech:

> 'I am afraid of the revolution which destroys and does not create. I fear going to extremes, the policy of madness at the bottom of which may lie the destruction of our civilisation and the coming of a terrible race of dominators who would bring discipline into the world with the cracking of whips and machine guns.'

The Fascists, then, were ready to kill and to die in fighting Communists. They were ready to kill to make Italy a new and better nation.

Work section

A. Test your understanding of this chapter by answering these questions.
 1. Why were each of the following angry with the government at the end of the Great War: young soldiers; wounded soldiers; nationalists; *Arditi*?
 2. What did the Italians mean when they said they had won 'a mutilated victory'?
 3. Why were Mussolini and his Fascists afraid that there would be a communist revolution in Italy?

B. Antonio Gramsci, an Italian politician, said in 1918, 'Italy has come out of the war with a vast wound, and blood pours in jets from a body covered in wounds.' Explain in your own words what you think he meant.

C. Study the photograph of wounded ex-soldiers. Then using the information you have read in this chapter, answer the following questions:
 1. In what ways do you think the men in the photograph were wounded during the war? Explain your answer.
 2. What point do you think they were trying to make in this demonstration?

D. Use the information on this page and on page 6 to write a short account of Mussolini's career between 1914 and 1919. Then see if you can find out about his life before 1914 from a textbook or a reference book. Was there anything in his earlier life which helps to explain his behaviour between 1914 and 1919?

5

THE EARLY DAYS OF FASCISM
1919 – 1920

Mussolini and his *Fascio di Combattimento* swore to kill and die for Italy on 23 March 1919. Their oath was put to the test just three weeks later when the Socialists in Milan organised a general strike.

Battles with the Socialists

In the afternoon of 13 April a huge crowd of Socialists gathered in the football stadium near the centre of Milan. Nearly 100,000 were there shouting slogans and singing 'The Red Flag', the socialist hymn.

Mussolini and the Fascists were gathered nearby. As the meeting in the stadium came to an end and crowds poured out into the streets, the Fascists formed into columns and marched towards them. When they got to Mercanti Street they met a procession of Socialists led by three women in red blouses and two children carrying pictures of Lenin, the Russian Communist leader. Gunfire rang out as the Fascists attacked them. Swinging clubs split heads open. The Socialists scattered in panic.

Led by the Futurist leader, Marinetti, the Fascists then marched to the offices of the Socialist newspaper *Avanti!* and forced open its doors. They threw the printing presses out of the windows, chased away the printers and set the building on fire. The Fascists then marched away shouting '*Avanti!* no longer exists!'.

This riot, or the **Battle of Mercanti Street** as the Fascists liked to call it, was their first battle and their first victory, but it did nothing to halt the activities of the Socialists. Demonstrations, riots and strikes became more and more common during the next three months. In May 1919 there were 316 strikes in Italy, more than ten a day. In June the Socialists set up a 'Soviet Republic' in the city of Florence. In the countryside, angry ex-soldiers marching behind red flags threw landowners out of their homes and seized their land. The Prime Minister took to riding in an armour-plated car while bodyguards took his children to school.

Italy seemed to be on the verge of a revolution. Then in September 1919 something happened which made the Italians think that the Fascists were about to take control of the country. **Gabriele d'Annunzio**, a famous poet and one of Italy's greatest war heroes, invaded the town of Fiume.

D'Annunzio and Fiume

Fiume was an Austrian port on the Adriatic Sea, just across the border from Italy. Most of its 45,000 inhabitants were Italian so everyone thought it would be given to Italy after Austria's defeat in the war.

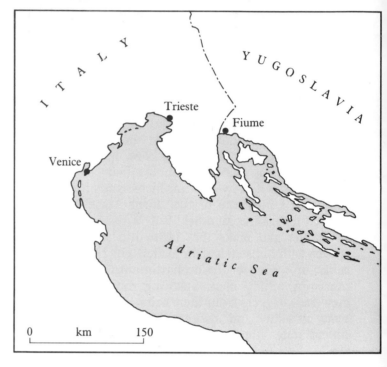

Italians were furious when the peace-makers in Paris gave Fiume not to them but to the newly created country of Yugoslavia.

No Italian was more angry than the famous poet Gabriele d'Annunzio. He was not at that time a Fascist, but he did have much in common with the *Arditi*. During the war he had made daring torpedo-boat raids on Austrian ships and he had lost an eye flying in bombing missions against Austria. Like the *Arditi* he now felt betrayed when he heard the announcement that Italy would not get all the land she had been promised.

Taking matters into his own hands, he made plans to invade Fiume and make it Italian. At the head of

One method used by d'Annunzio to raise money.
A Fiuman postage stamp

1000 well-armed *Arditi* he appeared outside the gates of Fiume on 12 September 1919. The small army defending the town gave way without a fight.

For the next fifteen months d'Annunzio ruled Fiume as a dictator. The people were taught to make the Roman salute and to shout '*Eia Eia Alala!*' whenever he appeared. But life in Fiume under d'Annunzio was exciting and young people came from all over Italy hoping to live there. Every day there were parades by the *Arditi*, firework displays, processions, concerts, mock battles, medal presentations. D'Annunzio got money to run the town by hijacking passing cargo ships and by raiding towns across the border.

Most Italians were pleased with what d'Annunzio had done but the government was unhappy. After all, d'Annunzio had taken the law into his own hands and was ruling Fiume as his personal dictatorship. So on 23 December 1920 the navy was ordered to bomb d'Annunzio and the *Arditi* out of the town.

D'Annunzio was wounded when the warship *Andrea Doria* scored a direct hit on his government palace and twenty-three of the *Arditi* were killed in fierce fighting during the following week. On 18 January 1921 they surrendered and left the city.

The importance of Fiume

Although d'Annunzio was defeated he had shown what could be achieved with the armed force of the *Arditi*. This gave great encouragement to Mussolini and his *Fascio di Combattimento* who continued to battle with the Socialists. D'Annunzio had also shown that a man of daring could use armed force to become the dictator of his own country. This lesson was remembered by Mussolini.

Work section

A. Test your understanding of 'The Early Days of Fascism' by answering these questions.
1. For what reason did it seem that there might be a revolution in Italy in 1919?
2. Why did Gabriele d'Annunzio and the *Arditi* invade the port of Fiume?
3. How did d'Annunzio's occupation of Fiume give encouragement to the Fascists?

B. Look at the postage stamp on the opposite page. What do you think the picture of a sword cutting through a knot is supposed to represent?

C. This is a postcard printed in Fiume in 1921 showing Gabriele d'Annunzio and his military achievements. Explain in your own words the pieces of writing on the frame around the picture.

Glory to heroes

Glory to heroes

Head squadron of 'Serenissima'; he flew over Vienna on 9 August 1918 (to distribute leaflets)

Commander of legionari; he left Ronchi for Fiume on 11 September 1919

G. D'Annunzio: poet – soldier

6

WAR BETWEEN FASCISTS AND SOCIALISTS, 1920 – 1922

Between 1920 and 1922 the fighting between Fascists and Socialists increased until Italy was near to civil war. The documents in this chapter give a picture of what was going on.

Violence in the towns

At first the fighting took place mostly in towns and cities where Socialists were on strike. Battles were often organised in advance. For example, warning of a fight was given when this notice was stuck up on walls all over the city of Bologna in November 1920:

A. 'On Sunday, women and everyone else who likes peace and quiet should stay at home. Those who wish to deserve well should put the Tricolour [*the Italian flag*] in their windows. On Sunday there should be only Fascists and Bolsheviks [*socialists*] in the streets of Bologna. This will be the test, the great test in the name of Italy.'

In the battle which took place that Sunday nine people were killed and nearly a hundred were wounded.

The 'punishment expeditions'

In 1921 the violence spread into the countryside when the Fascists organised what they called 'punishment expeditions' to fight Socialist groups of peasants. The next two documents show what happened when a punishment expedition went to a small farming town called Roccostrada.

Roccostrada was governed by a Socialist mayor who had been elected the year before. Early in April 1921 he received this letter:

B. 'Italian Fighting Fasci of Tuscany, Florence, 6 April 1921

To the Mayor of Roccostrada,

I, voicing the feelings of the citizens of your town, advise you to resign by Sunday the 17th. Otherwise you will be responsible for anything that may happen to persons or to property. If you appeal to the authorities against this kindly advice of mine, the above date will be changed to Wednesday the 13th.

Perrone Compagni'

The mayor did not resign and for two months nothing happened. But at 4.30 in the morning of 24 July, just as it was getting light, seventy Fascists roared into the town on lorries. For the next three hours they broke into people's homes, beating them

and smashing their property. As they drove off again at 8 o'clock, three peasants hiding behind a hedge fired on the lorries and killed three of the Fascists: the lorries turned straight back to Roccostrada. The newspaper *Secolo* described what happened next:

C. 'Along the road they met a peasant and his son and shot them dead. Then they ran into the town shouting "Who fired that shot?" They broke into several houses, stabbing four men. One of these, an old man of 68, was killed at his daughter's side. Three others were killed in the streets, fifty others more or less seriously injured, and seventeen houses reduced to smouldering ruins.'

During these events the thirteen policemen stationed in the town did nothing. None of the Fascists was arrested. The three peasants who ambushed the lorries were later prosecuted and sent to prison.

The methods of the Fascists

The 'punishment expeditions' of the Fascist Combat Groups did not always result in killing, but they were always cruel. Peasants were beaten with a long wooden club called the *manganello*. Men and women alike were given 'castor oil purges' in which pints of castor oil were forced down their throats until they were ill. On some occasions they were chained naked to trees dozens of kilometres from home. Women had their heads shaved bald. Men were made to eat live toads.

The Fascists were able to get away with this sort of violence because the authorities were often ready to turn a blind eye to what they were doing. Businessmen whose factories had been disrupted by strikes lent lorries to local Combat Groups and paid for the fuel. Landowners who were scared that their peasant workers would seize their land gave large sums of money to the Fascists. The police in many areas simply ignored complaints made against the Fascists and made no attempt to stop the fighting.

Even the government did little to halt the violence. Giolitti, the Prime Minister, could have crushed the Fascists as easily as he had crushed d'Annunzio and the *Arditi* at Fiume. But he disliked the Socialists and was happy to see them being slowly destroyed. For this reason, he supported the Fascists when a general election was held in May 1921. With his backing, and by killing nearly a hundred opponents during the election campaign, the Fascists succeeded in winning 35 of the 535 seats in parliament – not many, but enough to give them a say in how the affairs of Italy should be run.

12

Five 'Black Shirts' from a Fascio di Combattimento, or Battle Group

Work section

A. This cartoon appeared in an Italian newspaper in 1923. It shows a 'machine made with clubs and castor oil to punish false Fascists'. Study the cartoon carefully, then, using the information you have read in this chapter, answer these questions.

1. Why did Fascists make their enemies drink castor oil?
2. What were the clubs used by the Fascists called?
3. This imaginary machine is being used to punish 'false Fascists'. How can you tell from their dress that they are meant to be Fascists?
4. What do you think the cartoonist meant by 'false Fascists'?
5. Explain in your own words what you think the point of this cartoon is.
6. Do you think the cartoonist was pro- or anti-Fascist? Explain your answer.

B. Study the notice (Source A) that Fascists put up on walls in Bologna.
1. Why does the notice advise people to put Italian flags in their windows?
2. What do you think happened to people who did not put up flags?

C. Read the letter (Source B) that Fascists sent to the mayor of Roccostrada.
1. Do you believe that the writer was really 'voicing the feelings of the citizens' of the town? Explain your answer.
2. What does the letter tell you about Fascists' view of the police?

D. Using points C to F of the revision guide on page 18, make notes on Chapters 3 – 6.

7

THE 'MARCH ON ROME'

Fascist attacks

Early in 1922 the Fascist Combat Groups were re-organised into a highly-trained private army, or militia, led by Italo Balbo and Dino Grandi. The violence in Italy reached new heights as they attacked and occupied whole towns at a time.

In May, Balbo and 63,000 Fascists attacked the town of Ferrara and forced the local council to change the way it ran the town. In July they attacked Ravenna, burning the houses of Socialists and Communists. Before leaving they forced the council to give them lorries and petrol. They then used these as a 'fire column' to invade the surrounding countryside, leaving a trail of burned farms and beaten-up peasants behind them.

The Socialists replied to the violence of the new Fascist militia by organising a general strike in August. It lasted only a day, for Balbo's squads moved into the cities where workers were on strike and burned all Socialist buildings to the ground.

Mussolini's plans

While Balbo's men were on the rampage, Mussolini was trying to make himself respectable. He started

Fascist Blackshirts demonstrating in Rome on 4 November 1922, shortly after their triumphant entry to Rome

shaving every day, he changed his accent and took to wearing a suit, top hat, wing collar and spats. With this new clean image, he tried to persuade the public that he was not a violent man. In newspaper articles and speeches he told the Italians that he supported the King and the Pope and that he would make life easier for businessmen if ever he became Prime Minister.

But while he was reassuring the country that he was a man of peace, Mussolini was making plans with Balbo and the other Fascist leaders to march to the capital, Rome, and overthrow the government there. The government by this time was very close to collapse. It simply could not maintain law and order. The new Prime Minister, Luigi Facta, actually knew that the Fascists planned to overthrow him, but he could not persuade the ministers in his government to agree on a way of preventing it!

On 28 October the Fascists put their plan into action. Balbo and three other leaders set up a headquarters in Perugia, in a hotel opposite the police station and town hall. Mussolini went to Milan, close to the Swiss border so that escape would be easy if anything went wrong. The militia was ordered to assemble in three towns outside Rome where they were to form into columns for a march to the capital.

Rome under threat

The plan looked workable on paper but, in practice, it was unlikely to succeed. For a start, there were only 40,000 men in the columns. Some had no guns, only clubs. They had no cannons and there wasn't enough food to go round. To make matters worse it was pouring with rain when they set off and, waiting for them in Rome, was a garrison of 28,000 well-armed soldiers, loyal to the government.

Although the odds were against the Fascists, the Prime Minister took no chances. Facta declared that Rome was under siege and went to the King to ask for extra powers to deal with the situation. In short, he wanted personal control of the army to fight off the approaching Fascists.

The King refused, partly because he did not trust Facta, partly because he did not trust the army to remain loyal, and partly because he was afraid of the Fascists. Instead of giving Facta the powers he wanted, the King ordered one of his generals to send this telegram to Mussolini who was waiting safely in Milan for news:

> 'His Majesty the King begs you to come to Rome as soon as possible as he desires to entrust you with the formation of a government.'

In other words, the King was inviting Mussolini to be Prime Minister.

While Facta handed in his resignation, Mussolini took an overnight express train to Rome and was made Prime Minister the following morning, Monday 30 October 1922. The Fascist columns, which had come to a halt some 30 kilometres outside Rome, were then brought into the city by train for a victory parade through the streets.

The Fascists had come to power by threatening to use violence against the elected government, but they had not had to fire a single shot to back up their threat.

Work section

A. Test your understanding of 'The March on Rome' by answering these questions.
   1. How was the power of the Fascist Combat Groups increased at the start of 1922?
   2. Why do you think that Mussolini tried to make himself more respectable during the first part of 1922?
   3. Why was the Fascist plan to overthrow the government by marching on Rome unlikely to succeed?

B. Read this account of the 'March on Rome' which appeared the the *Daily Telegraph* at the time, then answer the questions beneath.

> 'The Fascist revolution is triumphant today all over Italy. The Fascisti this morning, when marching into Rome, were acclaimed by tens of thousands of people, and Signor Mussolini, called by special telegram from the King, has come to undertake the task of forming a new government.
>
> Italy is thus on the threshold of a new period in her history which, it is hoped, will lead her on to greater destinies. Mussolini, the man of iron nerve, of dauntless courage, of striking initiative and patriotic ardour, has imposed his will and personality upon the entire nation. Hundreds of thousands obey his beck and call . . .
>
> When the *Daily Telegraph* correspondent interviewed him two months ago he said confidently "We shall get to Rome", and today he has kept his word . . .
>
> Rome, Monday, noon. October 31 1922'

   1. Do you think the journalist who wrote this article was pro- or anti-Fascist? Give reasons for your answer.
   2. Judging by what you have read so far in this book, do you agree or disagree with the journalist's view of Mussolini? Explain your opinion.

C. A British historian, A.J.P. Taylor, has written that 'the March on Rome was really a comedy'. For what reasons can the March on Rome be considered 'a comedy'? Do you agree or disagree with this opinion?

8
MUSSOLINI'S FIRST TWO YEARS IN POWER

Mussolini with his bodyguards shortly after becoming Prime Minister, 1922

Forming a government

Aged thirty-nine, Mussolini was the youngest Prime Minister Italy had ever had, and he had to tread very carefully if he was to stay in office. There were only thirty-five Fascists to speak up for him in parliament and he still had many opponents.

Mussolini's first careful step was to form a government that would please most people. Instead of giving all the top jobs to Fascists, as everyone expected, he gave ten out of fourteen government posts to members of other parties. He did, however, keep the most important jobs for himself, making himself Foreign Minister and Minister for Home Affairs, in addition to being the Prime Minister.

Next, parliament. Two weeks after taking power he strode into parliament in uniform, spurs on his boots, and made a long bullying speech. He told the members,

> 'I could have turned this bleak hall into a place for my soldiers to sleep. I could have closed parliament altogether and created a government of Fascists alone. I could have done that but such . . . has not been my wish.'

Some members protested at this but Mussolini shouted them down. Then he asked parliament to give him full power for a whole year so that he could make any changes he wanted without asking for their consent. Even though it meant giving up their own power, parliament voted by a large majority to give him this power. Many members thought that Italy needed strong rule and they were ready to allow Mussolini the power to provide it.

No sooner had parliament given Mussolini what he wanted than he left the country to attend an international conference at Lausanne in Switzerland. His aim was to show himself to the world and to make the leaders of other countries treat Italy with respect. But although he strutted about Lausanne with an impressive bodyguard of Blackshirts, and treated people as aggressively as he could, no one took him very seriously. An English diplomat said that he was 'an absurd little man' while Ernest Hemingway, an American journalist, noticed him reading a book upside down at the conference.

Mussolini increases his power

Discouraged by his visit abroad, Mussolini returned to Italy and began using the power that parliament had given him. First he turned the Fascist militia into a private army to do his dirty work for him. Called the MVSN (National Security Guards) their job was to deal with his opponents. 'Must be beaten without pity', 'Must have his back broken', 'Must be bumped off', were typical of Mussolini's orders to them. At the same time he ordered the police to arrest opponents: within months thousands were under lock and key. And because the police were under Mussolini's personal control, he was able to make sure they did nothing about the acts of violence being carried out by the MVSN – five a day on average.

Mussolini used his special powers in other ways. It was important for him to get the backing of the Pope so he increased the pay of priests, ordered schools to teach religion, banned obscene books and made swearing in public a criminal offence. It was important to get the support of Italy's big businessmen so he reduced taxes for the rich and relaxed government controls on industry so that they could get on with making profits without interference. It was important to show the public that he was efficient so he made special efforts to improve public services, especially transport. Soon people were saying that Mussolini had 'made the trains run on time' and gazed in admiration at Europe's first motorway, from Milan to the Alps.

But what impressed the Italians most during his first year in office was the way in which Mussolini handled a quarrel with Greece. In August 1923 an Italian general was murdered on Greek soil while making maps of the area. Although the Greek government was not to blame, Mussolini demanded a full apology for the murder and insisted on a 50 million lire fine. When the Greeks refused to pay up he sent the navy to seize the Greek island of Corfu. In doing so, the Italian marines killed a number of children and made people homeless when they bombarded the island before invading it.

The Italian marines stayed on Corfu for only a month. The Greeks paid the fine and an international conference ordered the Italians to withdraw. Nevertheless, Mussolini claimed a great victory and the majority of Italians agreed with him. While the rest of the world saw him as a bully, the Italians looked upon him as the man who, by using armed force, would make other countries respect Italy.

1924 elections

After a year in office, Mussolini felt confident enough to hold a general election. But first he introduced the **Acerbo Law** by which the party which got most votes would be given two-thirds of the seats in parliament. So even if the Fascists did not win a majority of votes they could be fairly sure of a majority in parliament.

The elections took place in march 1924. At the start of the campaign Mussolini said 'a good beating never does any harm', so Socialist politicians were beaten up, tortured and terrorised. On voting day itself, Fascists rigged the elections in many towns. They confiscated voting cards from opponents and used them for themselves. They put the names of dead people on the voting lists and pretended to be those people. They stole the ballot boxes if they thought the vote had gone against them.

When the results were announced, it turned out that the Acerbo Law had been unnecessary. The Fascists had won 65 per cent of the vote and so had 374 seats in parliament. The other parties had only 180 seats between them. Mussolini claimed another great victory.

Work section

A. This Fascist poster appeared a year after Mussolini became Prime Minister. It shows (left) 1919 as a year of Socialist (*Bolscevismo*) violence and (right) 1923 as a year of peace and prosperity.
   1. Using the information in this and other chapters that you have read, explain what message you think the poster was trying to put across.
   2. Do you agree or disagree with the message of the poster? Explain your answer.

B. Make notes on what you have read in the last two chapters to help yourself remember the facts. Use points G and H of the revision guide on the next page to help you organise your notes.

Revision guide to part one

This revision guide is only an outline: it is not a complete set of notes to be copied. You should add your own details to each point where you see a row of dots:. . .

A. Italy was united in 1861 but did not become a strong country because of the big **problems** it suffered:
1. The problem of southern Italy. . .
2. Political problems. . .
3. The problem of the Pope . . .
4. Economic problems. . .

B. At the start of the twentieth century new ideas for making Italy strong were spreading. The most important groups with **new ideas** were:
1. The Futurists. . .
2. The Nationalists. . .
3. The Revolutionary Socialists. . .

C. **Italy and the Great War**
1. Italy did not join the war when it began in 1914. There were violent arguments about whether or not to join. . .
2. Italy declared war on Germany and Austria in 1915 after signing the secret Treaty of London. . .
3. The Italian army won few victories and was badly defeated at Caporetto in 1917. . .

D. **The results of the Great War**
1. Italy was badly damaged by the war. . .
2. At the Paris Peace Conference of 1919 Italy was not given all the land she had been promised. . .
3. Italian soldiers returning from the war did not get all the government had promised them. . .
4. For these reasons, many Italians said that they had won a 'mutilated victory'.

E. **The birth of Fascism**
1. Ex-commandos called *Arditi* formed Arditi Associations. . .
2. Benito Mussolini, an ex-Socialist, formed a *Fascio di Combattimento* in 1919. . .
3. The aims of the *Arditi* and the Fascists were to fight Socialism and to make Italy great.
4. Their hopes were raised in September 1919 when Gabriele d'Annunzio occupied Fiume. . .

F. **War between the Fascists and Socialists, 1919 – 22**
1. At first, fighting between Fascists and Socialists took place mainly in towns and cities. . .

2. In 1921 the fighting spread into the country-side. . .
3. The Fascists used terrible violence against their opponents. . .
4. Police and local authorities did little to stop the violence. . .
5. In May 1921, with the Prime Minister's support, the Fascists won 35 seats in a parliamentary election. . .
6. Early in 1922 the Fascist Combat Groups were organised into a militia. . .
7. By May the militia was strong enough to take control of whole towns and cities. . .

G. **The 'March on Rome'**
1. While the militia fought the Socialists in 1922, Mussolini began to present himself to the country as a respectable politician. . .
2. At the same time, he and the Fascist leaders planned to march to Rome and overthrow the government. . .
3. They began the 'March on Rome' on 28 October 1922. . .
4. The Prime Minister, Facta, asked the King for special powers to deal with the Fascists. . .
5. The King refused to give Facta special powers and invited Mussolini to form a government in his place. . .
6. Mussolini became Prime Minister on 30 October 1922. . .

H. **Mussolini in power, 1922 – 4**
1. He appointed members of several parties to be ministers in his government. . .
2. Parliament gave him the power to rule by decree. . .
3. He attended the Lausanne Conference. . .
4. He created the MVSN to get rid of opponents. . .
5. He took measures to get the support of the church and of businessmen. . .
6. He improved public services. . .
7. He acted aggressively towards Greece in the Corfu Crisis of 1923. . .
8. He changed the voting system with the Acerbo Law. . .
9. He held a general election in March 1924. . .

PART TWO

THE FASCIST DICTATORSHIP

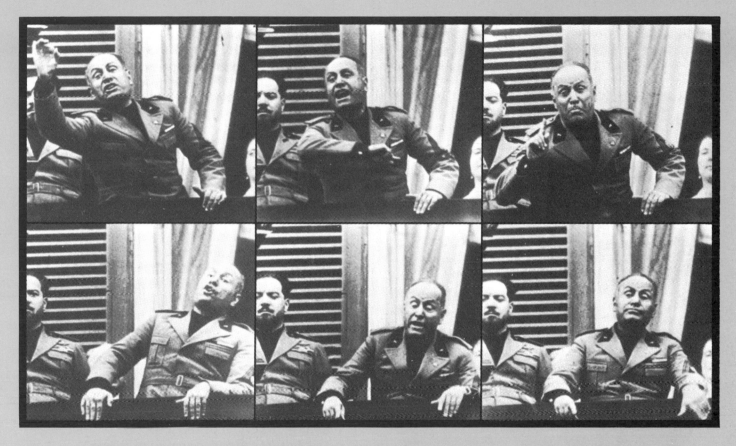

Until 1925 Italy was a democratic country and Mussolini was its Prime Minister, sharing power with the King and with Parliament. His official title was simply *L'on Mussolini* – Deputy Mussolini.

From 1925 onwards this began to change. He increased his authority until only he had any power in Italy. He made the King into little more than a figurehead and Parliament into a rubber stamp for his decisions. People called him by a new official title, **Duce** (Leader), and worshipped him as if he were a god. In short, Mussolini became a dictator.

Before you read about how he did this you should make sure you know clearly what the word dictator means. It is not an easy word to define because no two dictators in history have ever been quite the same. But one thing we can say for certain is that dictatorship is to do with power.

A dictator is a ruler who has complete authority: he does not have to share his power with other people. So in a dictatorship there are usually no trade unions, no local councils, no parliament. If these things do exist, it is only because he allows them, and their power is very limited anyway. The only organisation that might have real power is his own political party. But because the party is under his personal control, it always backs up his authority.

A dictator cannot afford to let people criticise him, for that would undermine his authority. To prevent criticism the dictator has a system of censorship; this means that he controls books, newspapers, films, radio programmes, and bans any that do try to criticise him.

People who insist on criticising the dictator or, more seriously, try to oppose his authority, are dealt with by a political police force. The police may imprison his opponents, perhaps torture or kill them, and they are always under his control.

People living in a dictatorship do not have all the basic human rights. They have only the rights which the dictator allows them. So they risk imprisonment without a trial; they are not allowed to speak their opinions freely; they may not be allowed to practise their religion; they cannot form their own parties or unions; they may be prevented from travelling where they want to go. They are powerless because they lack the freedom to do as they want. Only the dictator has freedom.

Finally, the dictator is often a 'cult figure'. This means that his ideas, his personality, his every activity are given maximum publicity through propaganda – posters, films, books, slogans, etc. The people are led to believe that their dictator can never be wrong.

19

9

THE MATTEOTTI MURDER

During the afternoon of 10 June 1924 **Giacomo Matteotti**, a leader of the Socialist Party, vanished from Rome without explanation. Six weeks later his body was found in a shallow grave among woods outside Rome, a pointed file buried in the chest.

Historians cannot tell for certain what happened to Matteotti because much of the evidence was destroyed soon after his death. But they do agree that it was a case of murder. They also agree that it was important because it forced Mussolini to become a dictator. It is therefore worth studying the case in some detail.

Giacomo Matteotti

The evidence

Most historians agree with the following sequence of events:

1. Early in 1924 Mussolini set up a special squad called the *ceka* to frighten members of the opposition during elections. A leading historian, Denis Mack Smith, describes three of the *ceka*:

   'Albino Volpi and Amerigo Dumini were professional gangsters used by Mussolini to harass anti-Fascist exiles in France, after which they were brought by him to Rome. . . . There this gang of criminals found that rooms had been booked for them in a hotel next to the Chamber of Deputies [*parliament*] where they were told to register under false names. The rooms were paid for and each member of the gang received daily payments from Mussolini's press office. . . .

   One man was specially released from prison by order of the chief of police for the purpose of joining Dumini's gang. He was asked by the latter if he had committed murder before and was then informed that their main job was to deal with Giacomo Matteotti, the most prominent opposition leader in parliament.'

2. On 30 May 1924 Matteotti made an angry speech in parliament, describing how the Fascists had used violence and fraud to win the elections held in March.
3. About a week later, the caretaker of a house in the street where Matteotti lived noticed that Matteotti's house was being watched by suspicious looking men sitting in a Lancia car.
4. At about 4 pm on 10 June Matteotti disappeared soon after leaving his house to walk to parliament.
5. On 11 June the caretaker of the nearby house gave the number of the Lancia car to the police. They quickly traced the car and found bloodstains on the back seat.
6. On 15 June Mussolini ordered the police to arrest Dumini and his gang on suspicion of murdering Matteotti. For the next week, Dumini was questioned by the chief of police. During this time, some of the evidence about the case disappeared and most of the *ceka* managed to escape.
7. On 18 August Matteotti's body was found. Shortly after, Dumini was sent to prison for murder.

You have probably noticed that one thing is lacking from this account of the Matteotti murder – the name of the person who ordered it to be done. The obvious culprit, of course, is Mussolini, but there is no certain evidence that he did so. Historians have therefore been careful not to blame him directly and some even think he was innocent.

The consequences

People at the time did not have such doubts, however. When Mussolini appeared in public the crowds no longer cheered him. Anti-Fascist slogans were painted on hundreds of walls. Many people stopped reading Fascist newspapers. Some of the MVSN refused to take orders. Three political parties walked out of parliament in protest and declared that they would have nothing to do with parliament while Mussolini remained as Prime Minister.

Mussolini tried to calm the situation by promising to get rid of the violent men in the Fascist Party. He expressed regret for Matteotti's death. He sacked three Fascist ministers from the government.

Matteotti's body being carried out of the wood outside Rome

None of this helped him, for the extreme Fascists now accused him of being too soft. Fifty senior officers of the MVSN staged a revolt. They burst into his office and presented him with a stark choice: either he must become dictator and rule Italy by force; or they would overthrow him and put someone tougher in his place.

Mussolini chose the first of these alternatives. On 3 January 1925 he went to parliament and made one of the most important speeches of his career. He denied setting up the *ceka* and said that Dumini's gang had acted stupidly. But, because he was Prime Minister and leader of the Fascist Party, he accepted responsibility for the murder of Matteotti. Then he finished by saying:

> 'Italy wants peace and quiet, work and calm. I will give these things with love if possible and with force if necessary.'

In other words, he would put the country back on its feet by ruling it as a dictator.

Work section

A. Read these two extracts from biographies of Mussolini written by well-known historians:

> 'On 10 June, Dumini and Volpi killed Matteotti and took the body into the countryside to bury it and conceal all traces of the murder. . . . The attack took place on orders from Filippo Marinelli and perhaps also from Cesare Rossi, the two leading figures in the Fascist hierarchy immediately under the Duce, both of whom regularly met Mussolini each day to know his orders. Not one of these men would have attacked the leading figure of the parliamentary opposition unless they were sure that . . . it was Mussolini's wish.'
> Denis Mack Smith, *Mussolini*, 1981

> 'At an anti-Fascist court set up in 1947 to re-try the survivors of the episode . . . it was suggested that the murderers . . . had not intended to kill Matteotti but only to beat him up in the way that they had beaten up his supporters and that his death was actually due to a heart attack. Certainly Mussolini's behaviour after the murder is scarcely consistent with that of an assassin or an accomplice.'
> Christopher Hibbert, *Benito Mussolini*, 1962

1. In what ways do these two historians differ in their opinions of who was to blame for Matteotti's murder? Suggest why their opinions are so different.
2. Judging by what you have read in this chapter, which of the two opinions do you find most convincing? Explain your answer.

B. Explain in your own words how the Matteotti murder resulted in Mussolini taking the decision to rule as dictator.

10
THE ROAD TO DICTATORSHIP, 1925 – 1928

Election posters encouraging Italians to vote YES for Mussolini in 1932

One month after telling parliament that he would rule Italy 'by force if necessary' Mussolini collapsed, vomiting blood, with a burst stomach ulcer. For several weeks he was unable to rule Italy in any way at all.

Shortly before collapsing, however, he had given the key job of Party Secretary to Roberto Farinacci, a vicious and bloodthirsty character who liked his reputation as the most hated man in Italy. He made sure that Italy would be ruled by force even though Mussolini lay close to death. On his orders, the MVSN began a new campaign of violence. One by one, leading Socialists were beaten up and in several cases killed.

Mussolini becomes *Duce*

By the summer of 1925 Mussolini had recovered and the opposition was quiet. He now took his first step on the road to dictatorship by introducing laws to censor the press. Overnight, newspapers lost all their freedom. From then on they could only print news that was approved by the government. Anti-Fascist newspapers were shut down.

The next step towards dictatorship came at the end of 1925 when Mussolini re-organised the entire system of government. First, the democratically elected mayors of towns and cities were kicked out of office and Fascist Party officials were put in their place. Then Mussolini gave himself new powers and a new title – Head of Government. This allowed him to make laws without asking for the consent of Parliament. It also meant that the King had to ask for his approval before appointing ministers. In this way both local and national government came under Mussolini's personal control.

With the press and the government at his command, Mussolini now began to create a new image of himself as a strong, dynamic leader who could never be wrong. People had to call him *Duce* (Leader). Giant posters of his face stared down onto the streets with slogans saying 'MUSSOLINI IS ALWAYS RIGHT' or 'HE IS OURS'. Newspapers printed flattering photographs of him at work, or riding horses, fencing, playing the violin, driving fast cars. Magazines featured articles about his amazing talents – claiming that he worked an eighteen-hour day, that he was a great writer, that he was a superb sportsman. Teachers told their classes that he was the greatest genius in Italian history.

Although this propaganda made Mussolini appear a superman, he was not yet a complete dictator. There was still a king and a parliament, even though they now had little power, and there were still opposition parties. This changed in October 1926 when an unseen gun-man nearly succeeded in killing Mussolini with a rifle bullet. It was the fourth time in three years that an assassin had tried to kill him, and he used this attempt on his life as an excuse to clamp down. He banned all political parties other than the Fascist Party and expelled opposition MPs from parliament. He abolished trade unions. He set up a special law court to deal with political offences and gave it the power to pass death sentences. And in 1927 he created a secret police force, OVRA, to hunt down his political enemies. They were imprisoned in concentration camps which were built on islands off the Italian coast.

Dictatorship by election

Only one obstacle now stood in the way of complete dictatorship. According to the country's laws, elections for a new parliament had to be held in 1928. To make sure that the Fascists won, Mussolini changed the voting system. Only men over twenty-one who belonged to Fascist organisations called Syndicates could vote. When they arrived at the polling stations they were presented with a list of 400 candidates chosen by the Fascist Grand Council, the party's ruling body. All they could do was vote for or against the whole list. If they wanted to vote for the list, they put a cross on a coloured voting paper, but votes against the list had to be put on plain paper. Fascist officials in the polling stations could therefore easily see who voted against the list and take measures against them later. Naturally the Fascists won this election hands down.

With a completely Fascist Parliament and a powerless King, democracy in Italy was dead. There was no one left after 1928 to oppose Mussolini.

Work section

A.
1. Test your understanding of this chapter by making a list of the ways in which Mussolini increased his power in each of the following years: 1925, 1926, 1927, 1928.
2. Which of these years, in your opinion, was the most important stage in the growth of Mussolini's power? Explain your answer.

B. In 1926 Mussolini ordered that this emblem must be put on the Italian flag:
As you can see, it is a bundle of sticks tied up with rope, with an axe attached to it. It was called a *fasces*. In Ancient Rome, the *fasces* was carried in front of magistrates as they went into court. It was a symbol of the power of magistrates to punish wrongdoers. The sticks symbolised corporal punishment, or beating.

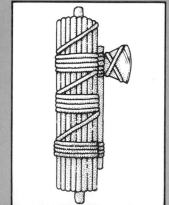

1. What do you think the rope and the axe each symbolised?
2. Suggest why Mussolini wanted the *fasces* to appear on the Italian flag.

C. Look at the photograph on the opposite page, then study the new voting rules that Mussolini introduced in 1928. Now answer these questions.
1. Why was it unnecessary for the Fascists to put up election posters like this in 1932?
2. Why do you think the Fascists put up election posters like this when it was unnecessary?
3. Do you think any voters in 1932 voted 'no' in the election? Explain your answer.

11

BATTLES AND CORPORATIONS: ECONOMIC POLICIES

As you know, Italy was a poor country. One of Mussolini's great ambitions was to make it rich. This meant tackling all sorts of major economic problems which no previous government had been able to solve.

Economic battles

Mussolini liked to tackle economic problems by declaring war on them. The worst economic problem facing him when he came to power was the terrible poverty of southern Italy and Sicily. He therefore launched the '**battle over the Southern Problem**' in 1924 and went in person to Sicily where he laid the foundation stone of a new village named Mussolinia. It was to be the first of thousands of new villages which would transform the lives of the poor.

In 1925 he started the '**battle for wheat**'. His aim was to get farmers to grow more wheat so that Italy would not have to spend money on importing it from abroad. The farmers who grew most wheat each year were awarded gold, silver or bronze medals in special ceremonies. Mussolini regularly appeared on farms, usually stripped to the waist, helping to bring in the harvest. Newspapers had to give massive coverage of such events.

In 1926 war was declared on waste land. The '**battle for land**' meant draining marshes and swamps, ploughing bare hillsides and clearing woodlands so as to increase the amount of farming land. The greatest effort was put into draining the Pontine Marshes, a huge mosquito-infested swamp near Rome.

Mussolini fought hardest to increase the size of Italy's population. The '**battle for births**' was an attempt to increase the number of Italians from 40 to 60 million by 1950. More people meant more soldiers. Mothers were therefore given generous maternity benefits. Couples with six children or more did not have to pay any tax while bachelors had to pay supplementary taxes which were especially high for those between the ages of 35 and 50. Newly married couples were given cheap railway tickets so that they could go on honeymoon. Every Christmas Eve the 93 mothers (one from each province of Italy) who had borne most children during their lives were given prizes. In the record year of 1934 the 93 award-winning mothers had borne a total of 1300 children between them!

Mussolini had a battle plan for just about every kind of economic problem. When the value of the Italian currency dropped in 1926 he began the '**battle for the lira**' to restore its value. There were even battles against sparows, mice and flies.

Above: Mussolini encouraging farmers to work harder in the 'battle for wheat'

Below: Mussolini and his wife Rachele set an example in the 'battle for births': their children Anna Maria, Romana, Edda, Bruno and Vittorio

Mussolini never really won any of his 'battles'. The town of Mussolinia was never heard of again, none of the thousands of villages planned for Sicily was built, and the South remained very poor. His only real achievement there was to put many of the *Mafia*, a secret criminal organisation, in prison after trying them in the special courts he set up in 1926.

The 'battle for wheat' was more successful, for wheat production nearly doubled by 1939. But so much extra land was used for growing it that the output of fruit, olives and other crops went down. In winning one battle Mussolini simply created another problem.

The 'battle for land' was mostly a failure. Only one area of waste land was properly reclaimed – the Pontine Marshes – and this was done in order to impress tourists visiting Rome as much as to create extra farming land.

The 'battle for births' failed disastrously. Despite the prizes and the propaganda and the tax incentives, the number of births each year fell steadily during the 1930s.

The Corporate State

Mussolini's favourite economic achievement had nothing to do with battles, however. It was the creation of what he called the **Corporate State**. He began building it in 1925 when he abolished trade unions and employers' organisations. In their place he eventually set up twenty-two 'Corporations'. Each was designed to bring together workers and bosses in similar types of work. The Timber Corporation, for example, included everybody who made a living by working with wood – carpenters, tree fellers, joiners, timber merchants, match makers, and so on.

Each of the twenty-two Corporations was headed by representatives of the workers and the bosses – plus three members of the Fascist Party to keep an eye on them. They then sent delegates to the General Assembly of Corporations which was headed by Mussolini himself, for he had made himself Minister of Corporations. This Assembly was supposed to make important decisions about the country's economic policy and about wages and prices. In this way Mussolini hoped to get rid of class differences and make every Italian into a willing servant of the state, working hard to make Italy rich and strong.

It never worked. Mussolini usually ignored the Assembly's advice and took the important decisions himself. The bosses in each Corporation always had a bigger say than the workers because experienced trade unionists who knew how to argue with them were mostly in prison or in hiding. And the system was corrupt. Friends and relatives of Mussolini and high-up Party officials got all the best jobs in the Corporations, and used their positions to line their own pockets.

Mussolini tried to make the Corporate State more meaningful in 1938. He abolished parliament and replaced it with a '**Chamber of Fasci and Corporations**'. This was a new kind of parliament which represented people according to the type of work they did rather than according to where they lived. But like everything else in the Corporate State it was dominated by the Fascists and had no real power.

Work section

A. Study these figures of the growth of population in Italy.

Population		Average number of births each year	
1920	37 million	1912 – 21	10,065,000
1930	40.3 million	1921 – 31	10,829,000
1940	43.8 million	1932 – 41	9,864,000

1. How can you explain the fact that the population of Italy rose while the number of births fell during the 1930s?
2. Mussolini's aim in 'the battle for births' was to increase the population. The figures above show that the population did increase: why do you think he was not pleased by this result?
3. Look back at the ways in which Mussolini tried to encourage people to have more babies. Suggest reasons why these methods did not succeed.

B. List all the different kinds of people who you think belonged to each of the following Corporations: the Mining Corporation; the Sugar and Beet Corporation; the Professional Classes and Artists Corporation.

C. Oswald Mosley, a British Fascist, described the Corporate State in these words:

'A society working with the precision and harmony of a human body. Every interest and every individual is subordinate to [*less important than*] the over-riding purpose of the nation.'

1. What, in your opinion, is the main reason why Mussolini's Corporate State never succeeded in creating a society like this?
2. Do you think it would be possible, in any country, to create a society like this? Explain your answer.

12
CONTROLLING PEOPLE'S MINDS

A group of Balillos parading through Rome

'MUSSOLINI IS ALWAYS RIGHT.' This slogan could be seen and heard everywhere in Fascist Italy. To make sure that Italians really believed that Mussolini could never be wrong, the Fascist Party had to control the way in which people thought and acted. This meant controlling all aspects of their lives.

Controlling the young

The minds of young people were particularly important. If Fascism was to last, the young must grow up loyal to Mussolini and to the Party. So schools taught them Fascist ideas from a very early age. Infants began their school day by saying this prayer:

'I believe in the genius of Mussolini . . .
in the conversion of Italians and in
the resurrection of the Empire. Amen.'

Older children learned about Fascism from specially written textbooks. This story is from the textbook written for eight-year-olds:

"'Teacher", said Bruno to the mistress as she entered the class, "yesterday Daddy bought a new flag. . . . Tomorrow we are going to put it on the balcony so that everybody in the street will be able to see it."

"I'm sure you will! But tomorrow all the balconies and all the windows will have flags. And do you know why?"

"Yes teacher!" cried the children, jumping to their feet.

"Good all of you! But let only Bruno speak. What is it tomorrow?"

"THE TWENTY-EIGHTH OF OCTOBER".

"And what is the twenty-eighth of October?"

"It is the anniversary of the March on Rome. The Fascists in their Black Shirts enter Rome and put everything in order. Then the Duce arrives and says 'Go away all nasty Italians who do not know how to do things for the good. Now

I will see to putting everything right. Long live Italy!'"

"Good!" said the mistress. . .'

Out of school, young people were expected to join youth organisations run by the Party. At the age of four a boy joined the group called Sons of the She Wolf, and was given his first black shirt. At eight, he joined the most important of the youth groups, the **Balilla**, named after an Italian boy who threw a rock at an Austrian policeman in the eighteenth century. The *Balilla* was similar to the Boy Scout movement, which Mussolini abolished in 1927, but the difference was that the boys carried guns and did military training. The *Balilla* code described the ideal young Fascist like this:

> 'He tempers all enthusiasm with iron discipline . . . despises fear, loves the hard life and serves with faith, passion and happiness the cause of Fascism.'

Girls joined similar organisations which trained them to believe that the ideal woman stayed at home and brought up the children.

Controlling adults

Adults as well as the young were bombarded with Fascist propaganda. Everywhere the walls were plastered with slogans like these:

> 'BELIEVE! OBEY! FIGHT!'
> 'BETTER TO LIVE ONE DAY LIKE A LION THAN A HUNDRED YEARS LIKE A SHEEP!'
> 'NOTHING HAS EVER BEEN WON IN HISTORY WITHOUT BLOODSHED!'
> 'WAR IS TO THE MALE WHAT CHILDBEARING IS TO THE FEMALE!'

If they went to the cinema or opened a newspaper they would often see long reports of Mussolini's speeches. These always appeared to be exciting occasions, for he took 'applause squads' with him to whip up enthusiasm in his audiences.

Even leisure was firmly controlled. An organisation called **Dopolavoro** (After work) arranged sporting activities and provided workers with cheap package holidays. **Minculpop** (Ministry of Popular Culture) made sure that films, plays, radio programmes and books glorified Mussolini and Fascism. The Party tried especially hard to control sport, for victory in international matches would show the strength of Fascism. Football was therefore brought under Party control and a Chief Referee with a gold whistle was appointed. Tennis players had to play in black shirts and give the Fascist salute at the end of matches instead of shaking hands.

The Fascist Party controlled time itself. A new calendar was introduced in 1933. New Year's Day was to be on 29 October each year and Year One began in 1922, making 1933 the eleventh Fascist Year.

Religion

Only one area of the life of Italians remained outside Party control, and that was religion. Mussolini needed and wanted the support of the Pope for his dictatorship so, although he did not believe in Christianity, he set about improving relations with the Roman Catholic church. He had his children baptised in church and then married their mother in church. He made swearing in public a crime, shut down many wine shops and night clubs, and allowed the cross to be hung up in school rooms and in government offices. Then he began secret talks with Cardinal Gasparri, a leading Vatican official.

In 1929 Mussolini and Gasparri signed a treaty in the Lateran, the Pope's cathedral in Rome. **The Lateran Treaty** gave the Pope 750 million lire in compensation for the land taken from him when Italy was united. It made the Vatican City where he lived into an independent state with its own small army, police force, law courts, post office and railway station. It made religious education compulsory in all schools and allowed the 'Italian Catholic Action', an organisation for spreading Catholic ideas, to carry on its work.

Mussolini thought of the Lateran Treaty as his finest achievement. He had healed the split between church and state which had lasted for over sixty years. This delighted Italian Catholics and made them more loyal to Fascism. It also meant that Mussolini could count on the Pope's support.

Work section

A. Test your understanding by giving short definitions of the following words used in this chapter: propaganda, *Balilla*, *Dopolavoro*, Vatican, Lateran Treaty.

B. Suggest as many reasons as you can to explain why Mussolini did not try to put the religious life of Italians under Party control.

C. Study the photograph of *Balilla* boys on the opposite page, then answer these questions:
1. In what way are they similar to Boy Scouts and in what way are they unlike Boy Scouts?
2. Why do you think Mussolini abolished the Boy Scout movement in Italy and created the *Balilla* instead?

D. *Either* write an imaginary extract from a school textbook like the one on page 26, teaching children Fascist ideas, *or* design a Fascist propaganda poster and make up a slogan to put on it.

13

THE ROAD TO WAR, 1935 – 1939

Many centuries ago, Rome was the capital of a great empire which stretched from Britain to the Middle East. Mussolini dreamed of re-building the mighty Roman Empire by conquering land around the Mediterranean Sea, especially in Africa. He said that his aim was to make the Mediterranean 'an Italian lake'.

War in Abyssinia and Spain

Mussolini began what he called his 'imperial journey' on 2 October 1935. Sirens wailed and church bells rang in town squares up and down the country. As some 27 million Italians came out of their homes to find out what was going on, Mussolini's voice blared out from huge loudspeakers, telling them that the Italian army had invaded Abyssinia.

As you can see from the map opposite, Abyssinia was sandwiched between two Italian colonies in Africa, Eritrea and Somaliland. Mussolini wanted to join them together to make a super-colony which he would call Italian East Africa. This meant swallowing up the Kingdom of Abyssinia. So while his voice echoed round Italy's town squares, the Italian armed forces were beginning the biggest colonial invasion in

history. Using tanks, bombers and poison gas, burning down villages as they went, half a million Italian soldiers found that they were often fighting bare-footed tribesmen armed only with spears.

Haile Selassie, Emperor of Abyssinia, went to Geneva to ask the League of Nations for help. The League did what it could by ordering countries to stop trading with Italy. But these 'sanctions' did not halt the invasion: no one stopped Italian ships from using the Suez Canal, a vital supply route, and no one stopped supplying Italy with oil.

As a result, Italian troops and supplies poured into Abyssinia and in May 1936 they captured the capital, Addis Ababa. Mussolini was triumphant. He had conquered a large country and he had defied the League of Nations. And he had got away with it. It seemed that nothing could interfere with his dream of making a New Roman Empire.

He took his next step very quickly, in June 1936, by sending soldiers to fight in Spain where a civil war had begun. Eventually there were 70,000 Italians in Spain fighting on the side of the pro-Fascist General Franco. They achieved little, however, except to capture the islands of Majorca and Minorca off the Spanish coast.

Mussolini leads the Bersaglieri Regiment in its famous running march, 1938

Friendship with Hitler

Mussolini's aggression in Abyssinia and Spain lost him the friendship of many countries, especially France and Britain. They began to see him as a ruthless international gangster. Only one European leader wanted to do business with him – Adolf Hitler, the *Fuehrer*, or ruler of Germany. In October 1936 the two dictators made an agreement to work together in future. Mussolini called their agreement the '**Rome – Berlin Axis**'.

From then on he was under Hitler's influence. In 1937, for example, Hitler persuaded him to join the **Anti-Comintern Pact**, an anti-communist alliance between Germany and Japan, even though Mussolini had always opposed Japan until then.

In March 1938 Hitler's armies marched into Austria, Italy's northern neighbour. Mussolini had often promised to protect Austria in the past, but now he denied ever saying such a thing and did nothing to stop the German invasion.

Another sign that Mussolini was under Hitler's influence came in July 1938 when he issued the '**Charter of Race**', saying that Jews were an inferior race. Hitler had been persecuting Jews in Germany for over five years, but Mussolini had never had any quarrel with the Jews in Italy. Now they were banned from the Party and from the army, forbidden to marry Italians, and prevented from going to school.

For a brief moment, in October 1938, it seemed that Mussolini was not under Hitler's influence after all. Hitler now had his armies on the border of Czechoslovakia, ready to invade. Britain and France were mobilising their armed forces, ready to stop him. Europe was on the brink of a major war. Mussolini contacted Hitler and persuaded him to hold off the invasion so that a meeting with the British and French could be held. Hitler agreed and the leaders of Britain and France met him with Mussolini in the German city of Munich.

At the **Munich Conference** Mussolini proposed that Hitler should be given a part of Czechoslovakia

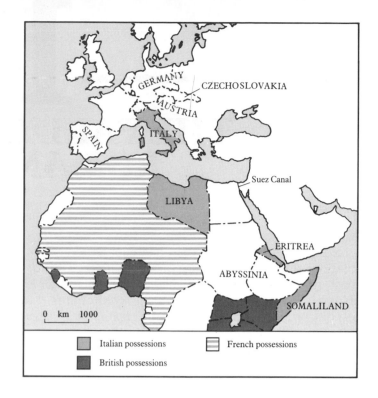

where many of the population spoke German. This was accepted by all the leaders and so war was avoided. Mussolini went home to a hero's welcome, people kneeling by the railway track as his train went by. 'I have saved Europe', he said.

But Mussolini was far from controlling the affairs of Europe. In May 1939 he made a military alliance, which he called the '**Pact of Steel**', with Germany: if war broke out, Italy would fight on the side of Germany. Although he warned Hitler before signing the Pact that he would need three years of peace to prepare for war, Hitler went ahead with secret plans to invade yet another country. On 1 September 1939, without consulting Mussolini, he sent his armies into Poland. Two days later Britain and France declared war on Germany. This time, Mussolini could only watch helplessly as Europe slithered over the brink into a second world war.

Work section

A. Study the map above, then answer these questions.
   1. a) What did Mussolini mean when he said he wanted to make the Mediterranean Sea into 'an Italian lake'?
      b) What would he have to do to achieve this aim?
   2. Suggest as many reasons as you can to explain why Britain and France ended their friendship with Italy after the occupation of Abyssinia in 1936.

B. Test your understanding of this chapter by making a time chart like the one below. Put the following dates into column 1: Oct 1935, May 1936, June 1936, Oct 1936, 1937, March 1938, July 1938, Oct 1938, May 1939. Write the events which took place at these times in column 2. Then write a sentence about each event in column 3, explaining why it was important. The first entry has been done for you.

Mussolini's foreign policy, 1935–9

Date	Event	Importance
Oct 1935	Invasion of Abyssinia	The first step in trying to create an Italian empire overseas

14
THE FALL OF THE NEW ROMAN EMPIRE

Italy at war

Mussolini often boasted during the 1930s about Italy's amazing military strength. He had enough aircraft to 'blot out the sun'; he had 150 army divisions with the most up-to-date weapons; he had eight million reserve soldiers whom he could call to arms within hours. . .

They were hollow boasts: the reality was very different. When Hitler invaded Poland in September 1939, Mussolini had only ten army divisions ready to fight. They carried rifles which were first issued in 1891. They had fewer than 100 tanks. The 981 planes in the air force had unreliable radios. There was nowhere near enough coal, oil, steel or rubber to keep the armies moving. Italy was in no condition to fight.

For this reason Mussolini did not help Hitler to invade Poland, despite the 'Rome – Berlin Axis' and the 'Pact of Steel'. Indeed he did not join the war for over nine months. Then in June 1940 he saw the chance of an easy victory with rich pickings. France was about to be defeated by Germany, so Mussolini sent his armies into the south of France to grab land there. Although they were attacking a beaten country, the Italians managed to advance only a few kilometres along the French Riviera. Then France surrendered to Germany. Mussolini had to bring back his armies before they had made any real gain.

In September 1940 he saw another easy victim. Britain was now under German attack so he ordered his armies to invade the British colonies in Africa. A month later he also ordered an attack on his old enemy, Greece. Both invasions failed. The Greeks fought harder than expected and drove the Italians out of their country, while the British army in Egypt took 100,000 Italians prisoner. Mussolini had to ask for German help. Hitler sent armies to North Africa to help protect Libya, but he also sent armies to Italy itself. Italy soon began to look like a German-occupied country rather than a partner in the 'Axis'.

1941 brought disaster to Mussolini's armies. The British defeated them at Tobruk in Egypt and invaded Italian East Africa. By May they had occupied it all and had put Haile Selassie back on the throne of **Abyssinia**. 250,000 Italians were taken prisoner.

Mussolini now had to rely on German troops to hold on to Libya, Italy's one remaining colony. General Rommel succeeded in driving the British out of Libya in 1942 but they soon recovered and beat him at the **Battle of El Alamein** in October. When American troops arrived in North Africa to fight alongside the British, both the Germans and the Italians were forced into retreat. The Axis armies surrendered in May 1943. The New Roman Empire had ceased to exist.

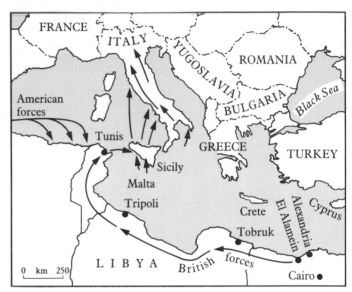

British and American attacks, 1941-3

Now Italy herself was in danger. The British and American Allies invaded Sicily in July 1943. The Italians put up little resistance for they were sick of the war in which they had lost so many men and had won so little. They disliked food rationing and they disliked the German armies which now flooded into their country to stop the Allied invasion. Above all, they were beginning to hate Mussolini who had brought these disasters upon them.

The end of Mussolini

On 24 July 1943 a leading member of the Fascist Grand Council criticised the way in which Mussolini was handling the war, and proposed that he should be removed from power. Five years earlier, Mussolini would not have allowed such a speech to be made and would certainly not have allowed a vote. But now he was ill and tired, worn out by constant defeat. He did not stop the Council from voting on the proposal to remove him. They passed it, 19 for and 7 against. The next day the king told him he must resign and put an army chief, Marshal Badoglio, at the head of the government.

It seemed as if Italy and Mussolini were both finished. He was imprisoned while the Allies invaded the mainland. In September 1943, however, German paratroopers made a daring raid on the mountain-top prison where he was being held. They took him back to Germany where he announced by radio that he would set up a new Fascist state in northern Italy, out of reach of the advancing Allies.

Mussolini's new Fascist state was called the **Republic of Salò**, after the town on Lake Garda where he set up his headquarters (see map on page 2). But he was no more than a puppet ruler with Hitler pulling the strings, and time was running out. As the Allies advanced slowly up the leg of Italy in 1944, the Republic of Salò steadily shrank.

In April 1945 the Allies captured the city of Bologna. The Germans abandoned Italy and began retreating across the Alps. Mussolini decided to do the same and, disguised as a German airman, joined a German convoy heading north.

Before he could reach the frontier a group of Italian partisans, or freedom fighters, stopped and searched the convoy. They quickly recognised Mussolini beneath the disguise and arrested him.

The corpse closest to the camera is Mussolini's. The men on the roof of the petrol station are partisans

No one knows exactly what happened next. It would seem that on the next day, 28 April, another group of partisans got hold of Mussolini, put him up against a wall, and shot him along with his mistress and fifteen other Fascists. The day after that, six of their bodies were strung up by the heels outside a petrol station in Milan. In bright spring sunshine, a huge and angry crowd took it in turns to hurl insults and rotten fruit at the swinging corpse of their *Duce*.

Work section

A. Read this extract from the Political Testament which Adolf Hitler wrote on 29 May 1945, thirty-six hours before committing suicide in Berlin:

> 'Judging events coldy, leaving aside all sentimentality, I have to admit that my undying friendship for Italy, and for the Duce, could be added to my list of mistakes . . . the Italian alliance rendered more service to the enemy than to ourselves. The greatest service Italy could have done to us was to have kept out of the conflict.'

1. What events do you think Hitler had in mind when he wrote 'the Italian alliance rendered more service to the enemy than to ourselves'?
2. If, as Hitler suggests in the extract, Italy had kept out of the Second World War, what differences might this have made to Italian history? Explain your answer in detail.

B. Study the photograph on the opposite page. It was taken in an Italian street in 1943. Explain in detail the scene in the photograph. Try to deal with each of these points in your explanation:
1. Why a framed portrait of Mussolini has been put up in the street.
2. Why the portrait has a bayonet and bullet holes in it.
3. Why there is a German street sign on the tree.

C. Make revision notes on what you have read about the Fascist Dictatorship. Use the guide on the next page to help you organise your notes.

Revision guide to Part Two

These note headings and sub-headings are here to help you organise the information you have read about the Fascist Dictatorship. Use them as a framework for your own notes.

A. The Matteotti murder, 1924
1. Background
2. Events
3. Results

B. The creation of the Fascist dictatorship
1. The Press Laws, 1925
2. The re-organisation of government, 1925
3. The abolition of trade unions and opposition parties, 1926
4. The creation of OVRA, 1927
5. The new voting law, 1928

C. Mussolini's economic policies
1. The 'battle over the Southern problem'
2. The 'battle for wheat'
3. The 'battle for land'
4. The 'battle for births'
5. The 'battle for the lira'
6. The Corporate State

D. Propaganda and indoctrination
1. Education
2. Youth organisations
3. *Dopolavoro*
4. *Minculpop*
5. Sport
6. The Fascist calendar

E. Fascism and religion
1. Improving relations with the Pope
2. The Lateran Treaty, 1929
3. The Charter of Race, 1938

F. Foreign policy, 1935–9
1. Mussolini's aims
2. The invasion of Abyssinia, 1935–6
3. The Spanish Civil War
4. The Rome–Berlin Axis, 1936
5. The Anti-Comintern Pact, 1937
6. The German invasion of Austria, 1938
7. The Munich Conference, 1938
8. The Pact of Steel, 1939

G. Italy and the Second World War
1. Italy's military weaknesses
2. The events of 1940
3. The events of 1941
4. The events of 1942
5. The events of 1943

H. Mussolini's downfall
1. His resignation
2. The Republic of Salò
3. His death

Revision exercise

A. Read this judgement of Mussolini and Fascist Italy written by a British historian, A.J.P. Taylor, in 1961

'Everything about Fascism was a fraud. The social peril from which it saved Italy was a fraud; the revolution by which it seized power was a fraud; the ability and policy of Mussolini were fraudulent. Fascist rule was corrupt, incompetent, empty; Mussolini himself a vain, blundering boaster without either ideas or aims. Fascist Italy lived in a state of illegality; and Fascist foreign policy repudiated [*rejected*] from the outset the principles of Geneva [*i.e. the ideas of the League of Nations*]'

Now do this exercise. Divide a page into three columns. In the left-hand column write down any four of A.J.P. Taylor's opinions about Fascism. Then look back through this book and find one piece of evidence that supports his opinion and one piece of evidence that disagrees with it. An example is given below.

A.J.P. Taylor's opinions about Fascism	Evidence to agree	Evidence to disagree
The revolution by which it seized power was a fraud	The Fascists did not seize power with their 'March on Rome' in 1922. The King gave power to Mussolini before the Fascists got to Rome. So there was no revolution	The Fascist Combat Groups already controlled many parts of Italy in 1922, using violence to get their way. So there had already been a revolution before the 'March on Rome'

B. Finally, what are your opinions about Mussolini and Fascism? Using the table of evidence you have made to support your opinions, say whether you agree or disagree with A.J.P. Taylor's views.